Aunty Della
&
Uncle Jerry,

On the road of "hap[...]
happiness, and "hop[...]
I hope you enjoy par[...]
& the book.

pg 69   Dedicated
         to gram's.
Love 'n Laughter Always.

Penny Dee - 08.

Merry Christmas

POETRY STEW

P.J. MCKIGNEY

authorHOUSE®

AuthorHouse™
1663 Liberty Drive, Suite 200
Bloomington, IN 47403
www.authorhouse.com
Phone: 1-800-839-8640

First published by AuthorHouse 10/20/2008

ISBN: 978-1-4343-8101-9 (sc)
ISBN: 978-1-4343-8102-6 (hc)

Printed in the United States of America
Bloomington, Indiana

This book is printed on acid-free paper.

IF YOU CAN RECONIZE THAT YOU
HAVE CHOSEN THE WRONG PATH.
~
THEN IT IS NOT TOO LATE TO
CHOOSE ANOTHER!

CONTENTS

A Poet An Environmentalist

A poet an environmentalist I try to be, hundreds of poems
written gone through twice as many pencils, twenty times
the amount of paper, sacrificing many a tree.
Poems written of poets, music and nature, written full of
emotion of hatred, love, marriage, kids, pets and death.
A few stuck in between to lighten the mood adding a dry
comedic twist.
Bringing up old memories, writing of other's plights and
struggles and the plague of violence.
A self-induced high the caffeine jitters, pot after pot of
coffee.
Fast food containers all over the desk, scraps of litter strewn
across the floor of crumpled poetry.
The constant blaring in the background a well of infinite
answers on any subject of life coming from the daytime
fluff on TV.
A river full of water, an over abundance of electricity and
the unforgotten sacrificed trees.
My environmental cares lost but not forgotten trapped in
the glare admitting from the computer screen.
Feelings of guilt yet self-accomplishment a goal set and
finished.
Digging deep and rediscovered myself, able to heal from
life's tolls.
My mind at ease my soul lost in a harmony of peace.
The coffee pot and the television are now turned off the
computer is finally shutting down.

I thank Mother Nature for her gifts for her inspirations I receive from her lakes, her rivers, her oceans, her mountains and her trees.

Focusing back on doing my small part of preserving the environment and wildlife for our future poets and their compilations of poetry.

The Poet

Paper on the desk with quill in hand he dips it in ink.
His words to be put on paper forever immortalized.
His words come easy, hard he does not think.
The story clear in his mind he begins to visualize.
Like a fast moving river his words flow.
A literary masterpiece ~ his words play out like a picture
show.
His words summed up in a few short lines.
A poem complete ~ his words sublime.

OUR SONG

Hear the silence of the night,
The beauty of the eve's light.
101 sounds of nature take into flight.

The crickets play us a gentle tune.
In the distance ~ the call of the loon.
The soft rustling of the leaves;
The song of the owl in a tree.
The sweet scent of nature, carried across the breeze.
The howl of the wolf fills the night sky.
Quietly harmonizing far off ~ the coyotes cry.
The humming of the insects as the fly by.

The music of nature sends us off into a deep sleep,
Hearing nothing but the peaceful choir of the woods, ever
so deep.
Playing our song… in our memories to keep.

KARAOKE STAR
OF THE ROOM

As the karaoke singer sings her song~
In her mind she envisions with her the world singing along.
The smoky lounge once filled with the clanking of beer
bottles and many conversations all around.
The crowd's eyes are upon her all glasses down.
Not one customer is making a sound.
Her heart synchronized with her feet~ as the drums install
the beat.
Not watching the words on the screen
Her talent is clear as she continues to sing.
The customers are amazed as they watch her perform.
The woman they know as the barmaid, their perceptions of
her now transformed.
Her vocals smooth, clear and strong, she sings it from her
heart.
Not missing a note with perfect pitch this song is her voice
part.
The owner of the lounge now watching his bartender
installing magic through out the room.
Not worried about the bar, noticing his customers with her
performance they are consumed.
The song is over the crowd stands and cheers.
Astonished by her hidden talents this girl that serves them
their beer.
Gracefully she thanks them, she places the mike back in the
stand and walks away.
Just as surprised by their response as they were by what just
took place.
She goes back to mixing drinks as if nobody just noticed
her knack to belt out a tune.
With one song she became the karaoke star of the room.

Isn't It

Isn't it fascinating how music can touch your soul?
Put a smile and warm a heart that has been cold for a while.
A person bitter and sad, actually smile.

Isn't it entertaining when people hear that certain beat of
their favorite song~
The young the old the weak the strong now are all dancing
and singing along.

Isn't it mystical and amazing the sense of power the lyrics
possess~
Affecting any emotion just by hearing the words of that
mystical tune.
Hearing just one chorus able to release your worries and
stress.

Music can be a beautiful thing in common we all share,
being forever universal.
Bringing people together joining hands in harmony~ a
friend, a neighbor, a nation, the world.

WHAT ARE WE DOING?

Surrounded by animals, art and nature.

Sitting quietly, thinking of the future.

Wondering where will we all be?

Destruction we caused to our earth and our seas.

So do we not notice or just not care?

Generations to come, how will they live?

In the near future, what will we have to give?

Will they have clean water, clean air?

Or will it be stories of the past to share.

Researching our wildlife that will no longer be here.

We have to stop, take notice, and make it clear!

God gave these gifts to show tender loving care.

ATHABASCA RIVER

Hear your rapids flow.
The autumn leaves reflect upon you hues of gold.
You've carried generations across your waves.
Centuries back, beginning with the fur trades.
The history you carry through the mountains and the
prairies.

Life, nature all around you I adore.
As we watch the black bears feed off your shores.
May your water always run clean and deep.
As you cut through land, mountains and trees.

A Morning on the Lake

Surface of glass, cold and deep, hues of greens
revealed by the sun.
Penetrating the lake's surface illuminating the once
murky now clear sandy bottom.
A school of minnows instantaneously head for
shelter in a weedy domicile, the baby's domain.
Here they are safe, their lives sustained.
The paddles cut through the water like a hot knife
in butter.
Leaving behind shimmering streams of silver,
dancing and swirling in the water.
Not a sound our movements make~
As the keel of the canoe cuts through the white
capped waves.
Bouncing off the lake the call of the loon.
It's cry held momentarily, suspended in the morning
mist~
Gathered around the cattails and reeds heavy and
dense.
Breaking the white wall a Mallard duck swims not
far from her brood.
We paddle on across this palatial body of water ever
so green and blue.
As we head towards the shore we inhale the
morning air.
Not saying a word to one another, both knowing
this was a notable morning shared.

BALD EAGLE

A hunter, a survivor, you're a commander of the sky.
Eyes of gold, face of white, gliding gracefully you fly.
You are a symbol to many, of freedom of pride.
To others you stand for courage, strength, wisdom and keen
sight.
Believing you create a stronger connection between
teachers, deities and spirit guides.
To me you are the majestic bird of beauty a breath taking
sight.
The bald eagle the hunter the survivor the commander of
the sky.

Northern Lights

Cold breeze fills the air` darkness blankets the sky, turning it into night.

Than a wondrous things begins ~ the northern lights take flight.

Illuminating colors of blue and green, waltz together across the skies.

Gliding, swaying, briefly blending together ~ as they streak by.

THE POLAR BEAR

Oh mystic animal fur of white, the great bear of the north ice.

The environment is changing, for this you are paying the price.

Your home is disappearing, is it to late to reverse?

You did nothing to us ~ this you do not deserve.

Progressions of people, altering this world~ your home.

Losing your food source and shorter shores for you to roam.

Your icy sanctuary is fading to the ocean quickly it melts.

Harder for you to make it, what a horrible hand you were dealt.

Your amazing strength and perseverance, harsh yet continued to thrive.

This battle served upon you can you survive?

Due to man's ignorance.. Some caring to late.

Now starting to worry about your fate.

Not many of you remain, how many of you will die?

Oh mystic animal fur of white, the great bear of the north ice.

OLD MAN MOUNTAIN

The morning sun breaks over the snow capped pinnacle
wall of mineral and stone.
The intense streaks of gold reflect against the veins of white
quartz and flakes of zinc and lime.
The shades of gray and shadows of dark accentuate the
depths of the crevasses hidden within your barriers of
infinite time.

Some need to conquer your great mass, shards of rock and
ice scaling the sides they go.
As their picks penetrate the tough exterior climbing higher
and higher.
To the heavens, bringing them closer.

Some desire to enjoy your wondrous offerings admiring
your rivers your lakes.
Casting their lines of hope anticipating for more than a
nibble ~ at your base they sit and wait.

Old Man Mountain you great prodigious mass the beauty
you manifest a peacefulness ~ that our souls demand.
A belief in Mother Nature's perseverance hoping her will
stronger than that of man.

ENCHANTED WOODS FORBIDDEN FOREST

I look upon you enchanted woods, forbidden forest.
The life you support, that Mother Nature created for us.
The sun shines upon you, showing us glitters of gold.
Your limb's so strong; yet so old.
Home to the owl the eagle the raven.
Providing them with a safe haven.
I look upon you enchanted woods, forbidden forest.
The life you support, that Mother Nature created for us.
Your branches reach out as your leaves touch the sky.
Twisting and turning, sheltering nature, you keep them dry.
Home to the moose the elk the deer.
In my heart I keep you near.
I look upon you enchanted woods, forbidden forest.
The life you support, that Mother Nature created for us.
You lived long about you many stories have been told.
Your life is in danger now, your future we need to uphold.
Home to the rabbit the wolf the bear.
Your life, your existence, we all need, give respect and care.
I look upon you enchanted woods, forbidden forest.
I respect the life you support, that Mother Nature created
for us.

THE CRY OF THE WOLF

The cry of the wolf is a sound all in its own.
A warning howl that brings the lost wolf home.
Off in the distance you hear a lone male's cry.
At the moon he howls filling the night sky.
Different howls mean different things.
For this one cry a mate it brings.
Hunting together they form a pack.
Taking the weakest deer down, the wolf attacks.
The wolf's sharp teeth at the throat it tears.
His kill is a good one with the pack he shares.
The coat you carry full and lushes of silver and gray.
The wolf's fur they are after, you are man's prey.
Constantly moving searching for a new den a safe home.
Due to man being able to hunt him, the wolf needs to
roam.
Not many have really seen one running, living in the wild.
To most they are scary animals from our books as a child.
The wolf's contribution that they make to the world is
misunderstood.
The help keep balance to nature, these creatures of the
woods.
So next time you are in the heart of Mother Nature, and
the moon is full and high.
Shut your eyes and listen closely can you hear the lone
male wolf's cry?

THE LIGHTHOUSE

You reach out from across the sky, protecting yet another
sailor's life.
Navigating them away from danger with a bright beam of
light.
The sailor's third eye this tower stands by itself here all
alone.
Built on this island consisting only of sand and stone.

It's view all around the depths of blue encircle the tiny isle
of rock.
Making some days not able to tell where the sky starts and
where it stops.
Above the tower and it's island absorbed with the sound of
hundreds seagulls cry.
As they fly overhead waiting to strike at their next meal
that swims by.

The sky grows dark ocean becomes a furious beast quickly
the hurricane winds moved in.
This is when the lighthouse and its keeper's job begin.
In the distance a tiny wooden ship being knocked by the
waves, sending off it's bearing.
Put it in a collision course for the coral reef known to
destroy large ships.
Captains all fear its mass know of its sharp shards that can
rip through any hull.
The stories told of the terrible sound it makes of the wood

tearing.

The tower beams it's beacon of light across the torrid waters
shining upon the ships bow.
Guiding the ship's captain away from the danger the little
ship was about to ensue.
Becoming once again the all-important third eye, protecting
another fishing boat a captain and his crew.

THE POWER OF THE OCEAN

The ocean waves come crashing in pounding against the
heavy melancholy that was left in the deeply embedded
foot-prints in the sand.
Pulling out within in its powerful strength the water cleans
the slate, removing all signs that were leading to the path of
despair.
The transcendental power cleanses the soul, purifies the
heart, reviving the thoughts able to bring an ultimate
peaceful bliss.
Leaving only a new path in front of you guided by it's
shoreline pulling you along, getting lost in a tranquil trance
from it's soothing sound.
Drowning out the any negativity on your shoulders you
bear in your heart you carry.
As the fresh salt water fills your nostrils lungs expand
filling with hope and desire, exhaling out your hatred and
regaining respect for man and nature.
Your heart warms your back becomes straight, as the
horizon now looks bright, removing the darkness you were
in.
The absorbent blue of the water calls you in, wrapping
you in its blanket of waves relieving you from the rough
dry exterior revealing only gentle softness as you float
suspended in placidity.

THE CAMPING TRIP

Pitch black is the nights sky the stars reflecting tiny flecks of silvery sparkling lights.

The call of a lonely loon echoes through out the valley as it glides across the glassy surface of the lake.

Crackle; pop, snap, a soothing sound, flickering colors of red, gold, orange and hues of blue.

Its audience captured in a trance by the way it gracefully moves.

Crack and fizz of the beer is the background rhythm that accompanies the drunken guitarist.

Wine induced vocals try to follow along forgetting the words repeating over and over the chorus.

Wieners are the main dish and marshmallows for dessert, their cooking utensils a simple whittled down stick.

The smoke swirls around their heads, a choke then a giggle as they pass around the perfectly rolled happy lettuce.

Out comes the Jack Daniels for the men and Butter Ripple Schnapps' for the women.

"Cheers to all" as they all suck back the three-ounce shots.

Some now envisioning faces and shapes in the glowing of the burning logs.

One from the happy group wonders off to regain his bearings, taking with him two beers and a drink.

With in moments he had fallen as he lay at bottom of the hill laughing covered in weeds, leaves and twigs.

Announcing proudly that he had not spilt a drop, still holding his beer and glass up with his other hand a proud thumbs up.

Now walking a little straighter the stray camper climbs back up the ridge finally reaching the top.

The park ranger stops in to come warn the unruly crowd, they have to tame down their fun they are getting a bit loud.

Walking towards their campfire he now clearly hears their inebriated rendition of Stairway To Heaven.

A look of surprise and a twisted grin at the unbelievable view before him.

As he rubbed his eyes, thinking it had to be the dark playing with his vision, this had to be a figment of his imagination.

As he soon realized his group of out of control kids was not that at all the youngest in the lively group was seventy-seven.

FLICK OF A SMOKE

A flick of a smoke the ash falls, with an exhale smoke
encircles her head like a gray foggy halo.
Far from angelic, this inconsequential paint of flat beige
dismal room.
No laughter, no noise just silence looms.
The living room setting~ resembling her life a blank space.
Others may perceive it as functional not stylish an empty
slate.
No color in the room, the same from within.
Same shape and size a photocopy of normality in the
background she blends.
Shadows cast never reconstructing no matter what angles of
light.
A dull view she has on life.

Inhale~ a flip through the TV. Channels, she's like a surfer
wanting hitting that wave hoping for the big one.
Riding it through until it is gone.
Disappearing like her inner self no longer a garrulous, jovial
independent woman.

Exhale~ a blue haze fills the room,
Sits quiet the woman, no expressions on her face,
independence buried deep yet still there.
Hidden in a place she no longer can recognize.
Her place here is important yet she forgets, without her for
them who would care.
Her presence is needed, for her they depend on, to them a

hero, their star in the sky.

Flick of the ash one last drag, your smoke distinguished.
Rediscover yourself dreams and ambition.
Open the curtains of your life, allow the light in, adjusting
your shadows.

With the last exhale the smoke it encircles her head like a
gray foggy halo.

A LABEL

Just do to a label ~ Bipolar in name.
People no longer treat me or look at me the same.
Treated as if my feelings no longer have meaning.
Unjustified actions… It's not always the Bipolar.
It wasn't long ago they all came to me for help for advise.
It wasn't long ago they said I can accomplish anything I put
my mind to ~ if I give it a try.
Now they avoid me, treat me like I have the plague.
Trying to hide their feelings ~ not always vague.
The media assumes put in people's minds~
People with Bipolar are dangerous, irrational can snap at
anytime.
Not all people with Bipolar are unstable emotionally
unequipped.
Many are successful, kind and gentle capable of
relationships.
So I ask you as a sister as a friend,
There is more to this disorder you need to try to
understand.
Some days I maybe angry, happy then sad all within
minutes~ spinning me into an emotional turmoil!
Please realize I may not control it, to me the symptoms
recognizable.
Separate myself from the situation~ I take on the roll of
Nancy Drew.
Sifting through the garbage and find the clue that triggered
the mood.

Many of times discovering the emotions are honest and true.
You would react feel the same way, if it happened to you.
Since having this label my life has changed.
People no longer respect me trust me not admitting they know me, acting ashamed.
Now look at me like I'm about to become that crazy cat lady that lives down the block, only acknowledging the cat's existence.
Her label from you, mentally unbalanced, basically insane.
The ironic almost funny about all of this is,
I've always been this person, as an adult, a teen, and a kid.
So you see it wasn't me that has gotten weird or has changed.
It was you, my people whose demeanor that has changed.
Since you heard of this label ~ bipolar in name.

Endometriosis

The dreams of having my own family most cherished.
The wishes for watching my child grow, with you I shared.
Once were so pleasant and full of love.
Are now filled with black hate and cold blood.
Visions in the day, realism and fear, terror at night.
The black tubes of death~
The old hands of pain~
The sudden end to a beginning.
The cold steal of a surgeon's knife,
Say goodbye to a mother's life.
The anger, the hurt, ~ when to have control of these feelings
and horrible thoughts.
Able to go on ~ Knowing your life time dreams are no
longer there. Feelings of being alone, abandon, empty.
Can they be forgot?

THE DARK

The dark cold lonely cloud moves above.
Wrapping around me surrounding me with anger not love.
One person's battle against a stronger self.
Throat closed, hands held down, can't scream for help.
Face drenched in tears…
Seeing faces, hearing voices from past years.

Frozen in the life I created.
One day loving it another I hate it.
The things I've seen, the person I've been.

Not always proud of my choices,
Knowing now I should of ignored the voices.
Not any better to listen and live by the heart.
Then people take advantage, tearing me apart!

Wanted to love again and not mistrust.
Try to carry on and not give up!
Ignore the past focus on the future.
Forgive and Forget…
All these words do take you further.

AGORAPHOBIA

People not understanding, a disorder from them you hide.
It keeps you locked behind close doors, never going outside.
Your memories of the sky and the sun still clear in your
mind.
Missing being able to go the store, panic attacks when you
try.
It was not long ago when you were always out having a
good time.
Until that day on the bus, a stranger crossed the line.
Taking your honor, self-esteem, raping your body your soul
your mind.
Not being able to walk, laugh or sing your happiness you
cannot find.
Wishing you could beat this feeling you have inside.
Wanting more than this window you look out, as you
watch the people go by.

BIPOLAR

How can I explain, help you understand,
That it is a daily fight, not to let it command.

Bursts of anger, hatred, sense of worthlessness, hurt and
tears.
Living and fighting alone, in this dark place for days,
months, years.
Always shifting changing these altered moods, I am so
afraid of showing.
Confusion, can't focus, the frustration, for you and I never
knowing.
Days of medication, trying not to give in.
Always wondering.. " Will it ever end? Is this all I have left?"
I would like to thank you for all your love and respect.
For always being by my side on this roller coaster.
Helping me take on the challenge, of living with Bipolar.
So I repeat myself, I hope you can understand.
Without you I could not win this daily fight.
IT IS I IN COMMAND!

WRESTLING OF EMOTIONS

The tag team of emotions step into the ring.
In one corner holding the heavy weight title, the ever so
infamous Anger, partnered with the dark cloak of Sadness.
In the opposite corner the challengers not new to the ring,
Hurt partnered with an odd never seen before in this arena
Joy!
Refereeing the match Mr. Never Sleep Insomnia.
The match begins first to wrestle Joy against Sadness.
Sadness is really pouring it on, Joy turns things around and
power drives sadness to the mat.
Sadness manages to slip away from the powerful opponent
Sadness tags out, stepping in to the ring Anger!
With a fury of madness Anger swings around climbing the
ropes lunges at Joy.
Joy quickly steps out of the way as Anger hits the mat with
full force knocking the wind out, Anger is disorientated,
Joy pins Anger to the mat, Mr. Never Sleep Insomnia runs
in " one, two"
Anger playing possum breaks the hold and turns it around
on Joy.
Joy is now being placed in a sleeper hold, too far for Hurt
to tag the partner out.
Then Sadness illegally enters the ring, assisting Anger in a
whooping to Joy.
Finishing off Joy now the focus is on Hurt.
Propelling Hurt over the ropes the two pound on Hurt.

Pulverizing Hurt into submission.
Clothes Lining Mr. Never Sleep Insomnia.
Grabbing the belts and still holding the title of Heavy Weight Champions Of the Bipolar Ring Anger and Sadness.
Awaiting for another match between Hurt and Joy.
Who knows who will win the next match, this one was a tight match for two underdogs!

THE GOSSIP HOUR

Daily you will see them, talking and laughing new stories
they bring.
Gathering at this park for the children, full of slides, sand
boxes and swings.
Armored with snacks, juice boxes and wipes.
Ready for action from the little tikes.
Sitting with the others, they begin to gossip and share.
Today's topic, who is doing what, with whom and where!
Tuned into the conversation not watching them play.
Not wanting to miss what someone might say.
Your child is calling you, requesting your attention.
Ignoring their demands with no hesitation.
A story of sadness of a marriage in shambles yet another
broken home.
You sit there and discuss your friends, your unfaithfulness
to them unknown.
Caught up in the moment you stab them in the back.
Like a mad pit bull their lifestyle you attack.
The hour has gone by now, your child stands before you
disappointed, and a broken heart.
Your time together was put on hold, spent on gossiping
with the mother's of the neighborhood park.

Righteous Brethren

Why don't you think before you speak?
What gives you the right to make a person feel low and
meek?
Who are you to sit in front of me putting down my
peaceful beliefs?
How can you justify of how you measure up all that you
meet?
Value them with what they own, what they have how much
money?
Why do you feel you have the right to treats other's if they
do not belong in society?
Who are you to decide who is uneducated a second-class
nobody?
Where in your heart can you justify judging and always
assuming the worse?
While every Sunday you sit there in church.
Do you feel no remorse when you hurt others as you reach
in the pockets of the disabled and the poor?
Not willing to return what you owe not only in funds but
also a kind word, a sense of humanity you deplore.
Are you unaware of hostility and negativity that hovers in
the large dark cloud you carry, shading all that is near?
The pessimistic attitude that you bear smothers any happy
out looks on life that others hold so dear.
You sit there and say you're a friend and will always offer
your support~
Yet your selfish actions and gestures tell another story that
cuts deep through a person's heart.

You refuse to address problems or keep any promises that were made.

How can you wonder why our confidence in you continues to fade?

You spout off what is right and what is wrong, preaching to others, as you place yourself above.

From what I remember of my bible ~ your acts are going against the word of God.

BRIGHT COLORS

Bright colors and light fill her mind.
Warmth and contentment fill her heart.
Her eyes tell a different story, sadness masks her face.

Her painting is vibrant the sunset so true absorbs you into
its glow.
The water so clear so blue; as the paint strokes trick your
eye~
The painted river appears to flow.
Then the oddest thing, the trees tall and dead, the objects
painted dark.

Bright colors and light fill her mind.
Warmth and contentment fill her heart.
Her eyes tell a different story, sadness masks her face.

Her pictures speak a thousand words, truth in the story of
abstract thoughts you will find.
Clear and precise through the blended colors of paint her
outlook on life appears.
Passion and love for nature the peacefulness she feels shows
in the colors.
The darkness and shades she creates seem placed were man
has disassembled permanently removing the work and love
the gifts gave to us all from the heart of Mother Nature.

Bright colors and light fill her mind.
Warmth and contentment fill her heart.

Her eyes tell a different story, a vacuous look masks her
face.
The woman stands at her easel another blank canvass is put
in place.

LIVING IN A BOWL

Like a goldfish he glances at the world through a bubble of
glass.
Seeing only what is in front of him not looking at the world
as it is, just as he perceives it to be.
Living in a circle of mirrors, reflecting upon him his
perceptions of life never to experience what is beyond his
castle or outside of his bowl.
Swimming in circles getting nowhere traveling the same
path day after day ~ treading water through out his
existence.
Never willing to swim upstream, stopping himself from
learning new things.
He put himself here in this watery grave drowning in his
self-damnation refusing to look past the world he created
this bowl of glass.

YOU KNOW WHO YOU ARE

Pretentious and pompous snubbing people as they go by.
Looking down at them on your pedestal so high.
Born into money with a silver spoon in your mouth.
Not knowing what hard work is all about.
Everything handed to you, the world at your feet.
Never having to worry about warmth, shelter ~ food to eat.
Can you reject your ignorance reject your hate?
Remember it was your grandfather's hard work, sweat,
struggles, that brought you your fate.
For it takes all kinds of people to keep your world turning.
You should take notice, life is more appreciated~ its there
for the earning.
So please remember this when next time you pass us by.
Life's not always easy, still we keep going, we work hard we
try.
Maybe reality will knock you off your pedestal so high!

A Shaman's Words

" No matter what color you are, or where you come from."
"When we enter into this world love was given to you, this
gift of love was given to everyone."
" Love makes all of us equal it runs through everyone's'
veins ~ for its love that we all have in common."
" We shouldn't forget our sacred job."
"It is in all of us, we all have the ability to show Love."

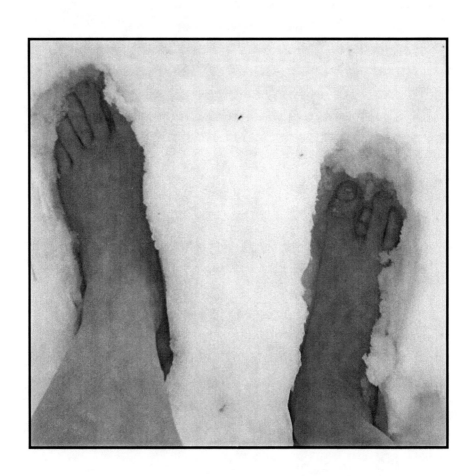

OLD SHOES

Open and enter the door of life, remove your shoes
shedding old idiosyncrasies and your forgotten flare.
There you stand at the passage of life your feet now
bare as your soul.
An introduction is in order it time for you to meet
you.
For years you were inflexible to try new ones
on, never removing those old grown use to too
comfortable shoes.
Made of thick leather smothering and enclosing
your free spirit your inner glow is dimmed no light
can get through unable to breathe.
Carefully you keep them polished to camouflage the
scuffmarks.
Still able to see they've been beaten they're worn.
The laces once strong able to hold it all in.
Now are frayed decayed and falling apart.
The strings are now wearing thin.
Every path you walk on wearing those old shoes
down life's path you're not able to enjoy the hike.
Cushioning your soul confining and an
impenetrable barrier making everyday, every thing,
every moment, remain the same.
Your shoes are the barricades that block the

experiences, not allowing in the compassion and
excitement you once had for life.
The rubber soul absorbs all that is before you on
your journey shutting out the world around you
that lies at your feet.

Shed those old shoes and sprint through the cold
recently fallen February snow.
Your feet now light and free barely touch the icy
street.
Your spirit is awakened your flare for life is alive.
A site unseen will then happen a smile will appear
your desires revived.
Your feet are bare; your inner light of your soul is
relit.
Your walk through life now happy and fulfilled a
positive anticipation with every step.
Now you are able to feel the warmth of the sand as
it heals your heart.
No more will you stumble over stumps and rocks.
With clear eyes you are now able to see what you
left behind you all your negative debris.

No longer ignorant to the true you inside,
You now see the world now full of pastures of
green, fields of roses and a clear blue sky.
Able to feel the textures you once knew pulling
them out of the shoes so heavy you kept in tow.

You feel the grass under your feet as you stop to lie
in the field of life you now appreciate.
Able to take the time to smell a rose your inner light
continues to grow.
Just by shedding those old shoes.

Answered Prayer

I said a prayer one night, beneath the stars so bright.
I prayed to let just this one come true.
That dream was answered   I 'm with you.

Many years we are still together.
So in love knowing it's forever.
Our lives so happy full and complete.
Thanking our creator for bringing us to meet.

Being able to have someone to hold tight.
Never having to experience a cold, lonely night.
Having someone with the world to share.
Knowing there will always be someone who cares.

In centuries before there were castles, kings and queens.
Now here we are, we have all this and answered dreams.
For our home is our castle, I his queen, he my king.

For all the love, joy and peacefulness that my husband
brings.

EVERLASTING MY LOVE

Everlasting my love, everlasting-
Whatever your virtues what ever your flaws
For you, hugs always passionate and warm
Everlasting my love, everlasting-
Whatever your mood sweet or bitter
For you, a kiss always supple and soft
Everlasting my love, everlasting-
Whatever your feelings fulfilled or disappointment
For you, my ears to listen, my shoulder to lean on.
Everlasting my love, Everlasting-
Whatever you experience young or old
For you, I will be here, by your side.
Everlasting my love, everlasting-

THE WISH

I wished upon a star ever so bright.
My wish was answered that April night.
You captured my heart, when you caught my eye.
Forever came into effect when you entered my life.
There is one for all, for a soul mate to meet.
My search is over for you make things complete.
You taught me of strength and love ever so true;
Showing me a world of happiness, I can have with you.
Pulling me in with the warm and gentle touch of your
hand.
Re-opening my eyes to the beauty of the skies and land.
Feeling the love pour in- to my soul, my heart.
You gave my life a brand new start.

WHEN YOU LOVE SOMEONE AS I LOVE YOU

When you love someone as I love you.
There is so much a person tries to show that their love is
true.
Simple and small gestures, love straight from the heart.
Try to show how much I miss you when we're apart.
By giving an unsuspected playful advance or a gentle touch.
A tender kiss, a note saying I love you very much.
The desire I feel to have your arms around me.
How my eyes express happiness for the whole world to see.
I am glad we take the time to say what we need to say.
Not being afraid of feelings or having to save it for another
day.
Working out any problems, of guilt, pain, or sorrow.
Knowing how much we want and need to be together not
just for today but also a lot of tomorrows.

THE FIRST DANCE

A stranger approaches and asks her to dance?
A shy look up she accepts feeling drawn to him at first
glance.
Gliding across the floor their feet never miss a beat.
They seem to match one another, already knowing the next
step.
Lost in the music the stranger's eyes locked their lips meet.
Never to forget this moment, the first time they met.

One year later driving down a back road being pelted by
rain,
He glances over at her and pulls off the road with a playful
smile he takes her hand.
Opens the windows turns up the music, in a complete
down pour the couple embrace and dance.
After the song is over they climb back inside and drive
away.
Both knowing it was the song they first danced to on that
Wednesday.

Four years later, there is a great celebration their families are
united.
A huge wedding all were welcome a hundred invited.
The lights go dim; the room is silent, as the couple walks on
the floor their first dance as husband and wife.
All eyes are on them as their guests watch this beautiful sight.
How much the couple is tuned to one another on their feet
so light.
Floating across the floor like two butterflies in flight.

Twenty-five years later people gathered once again.
A silver anniversary party arranged by the couple's three
now grown children.
They are all here to share in love of this couple
remembering how they met and where it all began.

Fifty years later she now dances alone.
You will see her every Wednesday night about 10 p.m.
She holds his picture close to her heart; casting a single
floating silhouette behind curtains of linen.

MY DARLING

I try so hard to get you to see,
I wish, I pray, that you would believe.
You think for you I no longer care.
I only want you ~ for life ~ our dreams to share.
Sometimes things may not go as we plan.
That does not mean I alone want to stand.
It's you I need, I want, to hold hand and hand.
Sometimes it may feel that our love is about to die,
In all honesty you still create a sparkle in my eye.
You still make my heart skip a beat.
I always knew you were the one to keep.
Our relationship may not be all laughs and smiles.
Do not forget on the path of life together, we traveled a lot
of miles.
My face may not show it, you think I am unhappy at times.
This does not mean that things are not fine.
Life can't be based on forgetting the happy and focusing on
the sad.
For you I will always love through the ups and downs the
good and the bad.
So when things don't seem right and you feel our world is
falling apart.
Look at me and look deep in your heart.
When we met our romantic fairy tale came true.
Our first date, our first kiss, that moment our sky went
from gray to blue.
Our love growing stronger as we go through the years.
Staying beside one another through the struggles, the pain

and the tears.
Through the hard times there has been a lot of good and
plenty of laughs.
So remember this my darling, my love for you will ever last.

MY LOVE

The first time I saw your face,
I could see the sun rise in your eyes.
The moon and the stars a gift from you, you gave.
To my dark and empty skies my love.
To my dark and empty skies.
I knew I loved you true, you I had no doubts.
I knew this the first time I kissed your mouth,
I felt the earth move in my hand.
Like a trembling heart, of a captive bird.
That is there at my command my love.
There at my command.
The first time I ever lay with you, that memory I hold dear.
I felt your heartbeat close to mine.
I thought our joy would fill the earth.
Last till the end of time my love.
To the end of time.

THE EVENINGS SONG

I sit here quietly listening, observing by candlelight.
The sounds all around are so calming this summer's night.
Watching you, loving you in the peacefulness you sleep.
You face so kind so gentle as you dream in your slumber so
deep.
The eve's song of Mother Nature's chorus comes into flight.
A gentle orchestra performing for the heavens it plays
throughout the night.
The music of tiny rain drops bounce off of the tin roof ever
so light.
In the distance the chirping of the crickets harmonizing to
the drizzling beat.
The trickling of the water as it flows through the creek.
The leaves create a wisp as the wind whistles through the
trees.
They all blend together playing for us all night long the
beautiful music of the evening's song.

How To Say You're Sorry

How to say you're sorry; not just the words to utter but also
your actions your behavior you change.
This way you never repeat the hurt~ you make sure that it
doesn't happen or have to find the words I am sorry again.
How to show that you love someone that your feelings are
true.
Even the smallest gesture of warmth and kindness through
a gentle touch will scream I Love You!

I FORGIVE YOU

I forgive you for forgetting your promises pushing them to
the side.
I forgive you for putting your desires ahead of the needs of
yours and mine.
I forgive you for turning a deaf ear on to my cries.
I forgive you for the distance you put between us creating
lonely nights.
I forgive you for hiding the truth behind your web of lies.
I forgive you for the hurt and pain I felt when you said
goodbye.

Please forgive me for losing my faith in you, in us, in our
love.
Please forgive me thinking you did not care for our
relationship enough.
Please forgive me for be being overbearing hovering over
you as if I was a mother and you were my cub.
Please forgive me for my insecurities at times becoming
jealous.
Please forgive me for the hurt and pain you felt when you
said goodbye my reply my actions seemingly overzealous.

I thank you for returning and speaking the truth, your
emotions you no longer conceal.
I thank you for taking this moment to pull me in close,
wipe my tears, for reminding us both that our love is real.
I thank you for embracing me tight holding me in your

arms at night, erasing the emptiness, no longer alone we feel.
Thank you for all your support and understanding, for being here through thick and thin.
Thank you for loving me and being my best friend.

We should not feel guilty for the words exchanged our near miss separation.
It was due to our honesty, able to listen patiently comprehend what we heard empathetic to each other's aggravations.
Bringing us here to a rediscovery of love, respect and admiration.

WEDDING DAY SONG

Every one has a special song,
One that they need to dance to or sing along.
That special song it can make you smile.
You know it word for word even though you have not heard
it in awhile.
That special song it touches your soul.
The lyrics you hear, love life you should extol.
Reminding you of that special day, you can picture it in
your mind.
When the first dance together you shared, the love in your
eyes.
Every time you hear it now, you begin to sway,
Picturing in your mind your wedding day.

THE WEDDING

Adorned with their mother's tea towels and good lace
tablecloths.
The tea towel becomes the veil, carefully draped the lace
cast a perfect white silhouette transforming into a beautiful
wedding gown.
Two sisters young, innocent, laughing at play propelled into
an imaginary world of happily ever after.
A metamorphosis occurs ~the backyard becomes the chapel
the sidewalk becoming the aisle.
A bouquet of dandelions and grass they envision baby's
breath and roses.
The fanciful organist plays loud and slightly off key, "Here
Comes The Bride" the wedding begins.
Walking to the alter, their father's tool shed, they float like a
feather caught in the wind.
The girls beaming at their guests of teddy bears and dolls,
in the proper attire for this occasion, all in their best dresses
and suits.
To this invisible man, not clear in their minds who he will
be, they are about to say, "I do"
A small factor, to them a minor technicality it can be over
looked.
No need for him to have a face or a name.
To them its about sharing and having fun playing this
imaginary wedding game.

Friend And Mother Forever

As the days slip into darkness, we see your face in our
dreams.
A wonderful mother, true friend, you have always been.
Your sweet smile and playful laughter your kind and gentle
touch.
The strength and love that you shared with us.

The way you held us when we were blue.
The way you taught us to be strong like you.
The hopes, dreams and desires you shared.
How you always mentioned us in your prayers.

We've seen beyond your surface beauty, deep into your
everlasting soul.
We have seen the purity of a child, untainted by a cruel
world.
Even though the nights were dark and your days were so
long.
You always found strength to carry on.

When a tear fell down your cheek, you feared not, for we
were there to wipe it dry.
You opened our hearts, finding there's a lot of you, with all
of us deep inside.
Whether it was night or day, you were there. There for us as
we wanted for you.
For you are our Friend our Mother… Forever True.
For all of this we say thanks and we will always love you.

A Father's Place

You took the time to teach me what you learned, what you
knew.
You took me to places nobody else would.
You protected me from harm when you could.
You were my coach, my friend at the park, someone who I
could talk to.
You were the shoulder that I leaned on, the arms that held
me when I cried.
You were the one I share my accomplishments with, proud
to say you taught me to try.
You were the one that took a father's place~
You're more than a brother to me, so to you I say~
I thank you very much, the admiration and love I have for
you, my words cannot convey.

A Precious Gift

She lies next to him watching him as he sleeps.
Hypnotized by the smooth motion of his chest ~ in and
out, in and out...
His air she breathes.
Drowning out the static tuning out the noise of the world
captivated by the amplifying sound of his heartbeat.
With a delicate touch she runs her long slender fingers
through his fine silky hair, stopping to play with one of his
curls.
Silently he wakes~ into his deep dark eyes she gets lost in
his gaze lost in his soul.
She runs the back of her hand across his cheek, gently
stroking his pale soft skin as her fingers absorb his beauty
examining every inch.
Carefully she pulls him close giving him a tender kiss.
This day she has been waiting for a lifetime to feel this
undeniable peaceful bliss.
Wrapped in a blanket full of hope and warmth.
Woven out of unconditional strings layered with a never
aching love.
She looks up from him breaking the spell her focus now
towards the sky.
She whispers under her breath with a tear in her eye.
"Thank you God for my son thank you for this precious gift
of life.

BERRY PICKING

Through valleys we traveled picking blueberries on a warm
summers day.
Forever in my heart that moment will stay.
I learned about your life the struggles you endured, how the
family stayed strong ~together they survived.
Coming from a family of strong women through out time~
How the men of our roots made their marks in history,
Doing as all did then~ just by working hard providing for
the family.
Many world events you seen at first hand,
From horse drawn buggies to watching television the day
they made that famous moon landing.
Being born in a different era five wars you've seen,
Amazing the flare you have for life after witnessing for
decades a world full of immutable beliefs.
The strides of life, your endurance and perseverance carried
you through,
Never to give up hope when it felt there was nothing left
you could do.
Just keep going and things will work themselves out.
It reminds you your alive that's what life's about.
Learn from your experiences, don't repeat your mistakes~
Appreciating what the world has to offer you and enjoy the
gifts of life what God gave.
Now I could see you and understand ~ where I came from,
whom I am.
It was that warm summers day I spent with the girl you

were and the woman you are I was privileged to meet. Thanks to our time together picking berries and walking through the trees.

GRAMS

In our memories you will never fade,
I will remember your laugh your smile.
The lessons you taught me, I use everyday,
You stood by me through every test every trial.
Daily I try to be half the person you were.
Your life you lived so innocent and pure.
Accepted your challenges head on, never showing the strain.
Near the end, always smiling through all the sickness and
pain.
Afraid to ask for help, your pride strong and always
remained.

THE QUILT

Stitch by stitch she carefully adds another square,
Using cut pieces of old clothes of yester year.
Each piece she adds holds a memory.
Each part she attaches is a story of her life's history.

Being sure that they hold the pattern in her mind
Creating a women's story in this design.
Adding scraps of her blanket, she was wrapped in the day
she was born.
Now a part of her creation of love, will keep her child
warm.
This quilt she makes putting all heart and soul is in it.
The baby kicks, carefully she adds another square stitch by
stitch.

THE PLAYGROUND

Now their fun will begin.
Summer has arrived again.
Children gather here in flocks.
Some ride bikes others run some walk.
Lots of time to play on the slides and the swings.
New friends to make, new memories it will bring.
No bad times here, nothing but happiness and hope.
Boys playing baseball, girls skip rope.
Oblivious to reality of the world around them.
Now they are pirates, cops and robbers, cowboys and
Indians.
Brothers and sisters no longer argue, here they are best
friends.
All the children laughing, singing, playing until the days
end.

A SNOWY HILL

Layer upon layer making your body stiff.
Can't bend your arms, your legs unbendable sticks.
Face and head wrapped in miles of the woolen scarf tight
around your hood.
Less than an inch for you to see~ ears covered with a layer
or three.
A nod of the head and a thumb up acknowledging
everything is good.
Hands in your mitts, one you can never loose, attached to
one another with a very long matching woolen string.
Mom guides you to the door grabs your boots then the ten-
minute struggle begins.
It's better to lie on the floor and give in then it is to try to
bend.
An hour and a half to get ready for that big day on the
snowy hill.
Suddenly it hits you, you're beginning to wiggle
Squeezing your legs together you can no longer sit still.
Mom recognizes this move, the layers she starts to unravel.
Less then a minute the last piece of clothing hits the floor.
Quickly you run for the bathroom door.
Your task you finished~ another minute has past.
You repeat the steps to get ready, with sled in tow to the
snowy hill at last.

GRANDPA LEE

Most people when they meet, measuring up, forming
opinions perceiving who they think you are at first glance.
Hair to long your carefree spirit shown through your attire,
wearing a coat made of leather, not of silk, most people
won't give you a chance.

Not caring who you are inside just looking at your outer
shell.
Blinded by the truth, not giving you the opportunity to tell.
Then he entered our hearts, stepping in bigger than life.
With no negative judgments, a free living soul his presence
always so bright.
A tip of his black fedora, a smile across his lips~
Blues music fills the background; he raises his wine glass,
and then takes a sip.
"Everyone has a good side even the devil has a nice red
suit!"
He would say with a giggle, then a clap, he extends his
hand, with in moments able to brighten anyone's mood.
Unfamiliar to them a friendly gesture was made~ the
stranger who was shunned that usually sits alone now
invited to sit down.
" Welcome to our friendly table, I'm known as Grandpa Lee
my man!"
The afternoon went on, the stranger now becoming a
friend,
Again Grandpa Lee was able to make someone feel good

about their self, now feeling like they belong.
Sitting there for hours laughing and sharing stories, playing
over and over 0001 on the jukebox, one of Grandpa's
favorite songs.
The two once sat alone now the table is full.
Their time together just flying by now it's close to last call.
This was a familiar scene whenever Grandpa Lee was here.
Everyone always gravitated to him knowing happiness and
a joy for life was near.

THE LIFE OF A GREAT MAN

His weak white hand reached across the table
embracing mine.
As his words of wisdom poured out I could see him
transform.
Stricken with cancer; no longer seemed weak and
worn.
His eyes lit up as he began to share his story,
It was a live version of past world events and his part
in history.
As a young man he became a zoot suiter going
against the grain of society.
A group of youngsters traveling the streets, dancing
and grooving to that forbidden music called jazz.
A sip of Mogan David he continued on about his
past,
Mentioning briefly about war he lived through ~
and the ironic circumstances behind his maiming
injury.
He sustained from the war of peace that broke out
on his street.
For a moment you could see his heart break as he
spoke of his one true love.

He spoke of her golden hair, her soothing voice, and her soft and gentle touch.
The home they built the children they raised the happiness the shared.
How she was the final chapter of his love life~
After she left he never thought of seeking another wife.
He spoke of always finding music in your heart it will get you through life even the hard parts.
There is a song for any feeling or situation it is just a point of changing the station.
If you live your life as you control your radio, your heart and mind will always heal.
After that day I made sure I visited with him every night.
Listening to the stories he loved to share of his life.
No matter how sick he was at the end.
He always made time to share with a friend.
He touched my heart he touched my soul.
I will never forget the stories he told.
I will always remember the life of this great man.

CALDER KIDS

Everyone had his or her place, sitting in the same order
grade after grade.
Growing together their tight knit group.
Sharing in one another's growing pains, they were always
together always having someone to talk to.
A mishmash of blended personalities not noticing one
another beliefs or race.
To them it did not matter all they seen was a friend.
All of the children had a lot of things in common.
The color of blood their flare for life and the love for the
tiny neighborhood.
Their behaviors slightly differed from other children their
attitude and school unique.
It was there that many of them found happiness and a sense
of peace.
Knowing that at the end of the day they return back to
their chaotic environments they lived in.
As soon as they stepped through the front door their
individual horrors began.
Some returned to homes that ran on alcohol and drugs.
Some homes were full of siblings with morsels of food no
warmth no water for the tub.
Hard working parents who struggled just could not earn
enough.
Some were from homes of silence disguising the physical
and sexual abuse by the white picket fences they lived
behind.
Some of them came from homes of constant arguing no

quiet area for them to escape, as they heard their parents
yelling through out the night.
Some homes were full of joy and laughter but no stability
their parents never home their children were always left
alone.
Leaving a seven year old to do the job of taking care of two
smaller children and a newborn.
Some came from homes of order and control no room for
free spirited children.
Their home life was built on strict structure, no talking no
exploring of the imagination.
A rigid routine of reading then music studies no time for
play; only time for practicing the violin.

Quickly following a regimented diet at 6:50 p.m. they are
carted off to bed.
All of these children found a way of tuning out the
negativity and sadness that surrounded them.
As they envisioned the day they shared at school at recess in
the park.
Each memory each moment spent with their friends they
hold on to joy pulling them out of their tiny worlds of
dark.
They discovered together the sun the moon and the stars
where life began how fires start.
Learning together how to write read sing and dance.
Growing older together more curious now their
imaginations advanced.
This is where they discovered their first crush first kiss.
All within these hallowed halls of their school made of red
brick.
As they got older some families separated others moved to

have a fresh start.
The group of friends slowly fell apart.
Forever holding on to one another by memory~ remaining together in their hearts.
The love and respect for one another never faltered, some still get together and reminisce about the experiences they shared in Calder.

THE HIGH SCHOOL BATHROOM

Groups of them in their own little clicks to this room they
congregate.
Their private oasis~ where important issues are discussed,
the day's plans made.
The room clean and stark consisting of toilet stalls, rows of
mirrors and sinks.
A group of teen girls check their hair and faces, their eyes
locked on self- image~ forever worried what others may
think.
The preppy girls whisper about the tomboys, whom refused
cosmetology for shop.
The rebellious girls standing by the stalls, snub the rules,
pull out their smokes and light up.
The shy girl in the corner just wanting to fit in, lost for
words she awkwardly stammers not knowing where to
begin.
The spirited cheerleaders come in bouncing, always hyper
and full of pep.
At their presence the gothic girls grind their teeth with
nefarious grins envisioning a tragic pyramid death.
No matter their differences, one thing they all have in
common,
In this high school bathroom is where their lives begin to
change, in here women they all become.

DARK HAIRED BEAUTY

Curls and waves my dark haired beauty.
Eyes piercing brown, sometimes looking right through me.
The love I have for you the happiness to my life you bring.
Unconditional love, only wanting one thing.

Turning from me you walk away.
Bringing back the ball you want to play.
A wag of your tail your ears perk up.
Still full of energy my five year old pup.

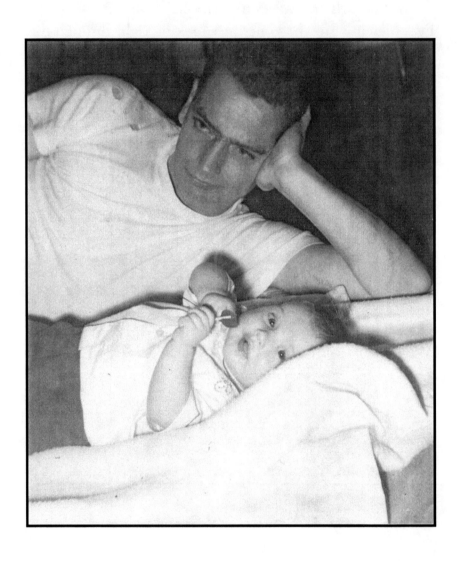

DAD

My life changed that dark September day.
Still so young, when you went away.
So many things left to share with you, still so much to say.
I was just getting to know you, know me.
Wanting to know more, who you are and used to be.
Barely knowing our family, I feel I am missing pieces.
All the brothers, sisters, aunts, uncles, cousins, nephews,
nieces.
You had a whole other life before I arrived.
So many questions, too many different answers, what is the
truth what is lies.
Things people will not tell me, things about you they hide.
I want to know whom we are as people, where we came
from, our family history.
Things you liked, art, music, to your favorite thing on TV.
Simple things ~ not the negative impact that caused a break
in the family.
So I keep your picture close, cherishing the happy
memories.
Times it was just us, walking, talking, and laughing your
smile I remember.
My eyes tear up now thinking of you father, wishing I never
lost you that dark day of September.

THE DEATH BED

All heads down, a family so separated, so distant to one
another,
Now all embraced arms linked, mother, sisters, brothers.
As they are gathered around his bed an anomalous silence
fills the room.
Another chapter of life has ended, feeling a smothering
sense of loss and gloom.
His stepdaughter that from him seemed the furthest, always
lost in the family dynamics, now sits by his side, not being
able to let go of his hand.
Whispers the words "I love you and I was lucky to have you
as a dad."
Letting go of all the hurt of the past.
He grasps her hand, his eyes slightly open, a weak smile he
whispers back.
" You're my daughter, you will do just fine in life, goodbye
my girl goodbye."
A single tear runs down his cheek, a small breath he takes,
his hand grows limp and drops next to his side.
This will be the last time they see him together as a family
they now just realize.
His stepdaughter finally finding out what she already knew
deep down inside.
More than a father was lost that day.
A family a chance to come together instead threw it away,
all going their separate ways.
Except for the stepchildren he raised by their mother's side

they stayed.
A final hug, a kiss, still holding their father close, on
bended knee together for him the three silently prayed.

YOUR BEAM OF LIGHT

This road of life that I have traveled the things I have seen,
Has brought me to this place, no regrets of where I have
been.
Going new places, meeting new people, not afraid to try
new things.
Many memories of good and bad my travels did bring.
Living quite a colorful life, hit some bumps along the way.
Always was able to bounce back at the end of the day.
Remember that life I did live, on this day do not shed a
tear.
For my smile will always be with you, in your memories I
am here.
Please know it was you that made my life fulfilled and
complete.
So my family my friends this not good bye, someday again
we'll meet.
So ask you to go on, be happy do not be afraid to follow
your dreams.
Let the sun and moon light your path, for I will be with
you, I will be your beam.
So today I start I am your beam of light, I bring you out of
the dark.
Remember my face, my laugh; I will always be forever in
your heart.

Forty Years And Still Going

Peace and love make love not war.
A generation of hope in an eve of destruction a nation was torn.
Another hit another pull rooms filled with a purple haze.
Psychedelic colors the world sways in front of them moving at a slow pace.
A sense of calmness fills the air as they adjust the flowers in their hair.
Progression of science skyrockets as the world watches mans first steps on the moon.
The decade ended goodbye to Jim, Jimi and Janis, the disco era we ensued.

Ball made of mirror hung over the dance floor, on this ruby Tuesday the boogie night of the bullfrog blues.
The occupants fashioned in silk shirts bell-bottoms and platform shoes.
While others were rexing on roller-skates on spinning wheels they groove.
A generation of kids believing they'd make it through the hustle of life taking a chance on their future for the need to dance.
The era ended by being pulled into a disco inferno fading into a boogie wonderland never to return these disco nights.

No more smoking in the boy's room, school is out for the

summer heavy metal blaring unable to drive 55 on the
highway of life.
Backcombed mullets dowsed in gel then mousse then held
up with hair spray.
Studded dog collars, animal print spandex layered with
leather and lace.
Material girls hooking up with urban cowboys, competing
against the yuppies that are trying to keep up with the
Joneses, who will win this race.
Taking it to the limit the end of a decade the yuppies are
running on empty their steps behind them fade.

You see them now hand in pockets sipping on a decaf' no
sugar skim milk extra foam latte.
While across the world not even half way, a society is
reborn.
Stone by stone as they brought down the wall.

November rains came three months late bringing an end to
the storm,
The water washed away the sand that collected on the
troops souls into a bed of roses the dirt falls.

A new decade a new view on life our windows altered now
computerized electronically framed.
Leaving us behind ashes and dust, good riddance is applied
in their waves leaving most of us standing still as they sprint
by us in life's race.
Donald Trump, Bill Gates and Ross Perreaux are the top
three in the lead.
One dropping out of the race, a nation reminding him he
could not buy the presidency.

With arms wide open welcoming a new decade.
The world celebrates the eve of Y2K.
One step closer and able to breathe Mr. Trump regains the lead.
The hair club for men he is in dire need.
Still he manages to star as himself on reality TV.
Bill Gates taking a bite out of the apple continues to stay in the race of commanding the grip on technology.

Like rolling stones we continue on with no satisfaction from the outcome.
Like a pack of wild horses we seek a never-ending supply of lush pastures of green.
Not stopping to see the big picture to afraid to slow down and soak up the sun.
As the race continues on~

The track is a forever-winding road of life.
Sometimes we cruise by the past bringing back the styles mimic the voices that holds our thoughts never to forget the wisdom they brought.
We still struggle and fight for human kindness human rights.
Now adding to our cause of our global warming plight.

Innocent free speech blogs filled pathways of shared beliefs.
Bringing new friends new love into our lives instantly traveling over miles of land and across great big seas.
Coming together through an Internet link with a touch of a key.

OPENING NIGHT

Script memorized ~ ready for action like a well trained
solider, you take your place.
The performing artist armoured with confidence and
aptitude.
The lights in the theatre go dim, the spot light illuminates
center stage.
Separate yourself from yourself, to develop into..
Forming yourself, like a child molding playdoh, forcing the
shapes the image comes alive.
Your skills bright and vibrant, tonight your performance
will thrive.
The playwright has an incurable optimistic faith in his
words.
If it's a flop a mockery of the theatre, blame turns; it's the
director's error.
It was his rendition of the play, his choice of the lead actor.
It's your adroitness that carries the character, bringing it to
life.
First act, second, third and last!
The curtain falls another performance you got through.
Armoured with confidence and aptitude.
Delivering success to open night.

THE OLD MUD SHACK

Skies of blue is your backdrop ~ surrounded by majestic
trees and fields of green:
Words cannot describe this picture so pristine.

Standing alone in fields of wildflowers, embracing your
frame.
Some curtains still hanging behind your cracked
windowpanes.
Old lumber broken and decayed, the history you carried
still remains.

The wind whistles threw you now, weather beaten and
worn.
How many stories can you tell? These walls once adorn.
The walls that once kept a family safe dry and warm.

The work and love they put into building you ~ once their
happy home.
A place where people could gather, never to feel alone.

Looking at you takes me back…
I can smell the dinner cooking and the children laugh.
So thank you for this moment, for taking me back to the
past.

To me you were a home and not an old mud shack.

THE CARNIVAL

Set up, tear down, spring is here their work season begins.
Constantly on the move, for weeks on end!
From one spot to another~ not much sleep in between.
They work well together like a well-oiled machine.
Set up the stick joints, stock up the stuffies.
Ride jocks busy~ rise of the Super Loop ~ with no
difficulty.
The gates are about to open tickets ready to sell.
What kind of day will they have, no carnie can tell.
The grounds are starting to fill, walking down the joint line.
Joint liners announcing the game, as they walk by.
Shouting at the unsuspected customers to step up, to step
in.
Convincing them it is easy, they are guaranteed of the big
win.
Ride jocks are pumped now, the ride is running, music
playing, and they're ready to go.
They know this is what brings the crowds in; their rides are
a main part of the show.
Cotton candy, mini doughnuts, candy apples made and
ready eat.
More than just children gather for these sweet treats.
The sunsets behind them, it is getting dark.
Hundreds people gather now waiting for the fireworks to
start.
The night is over the show is closed, It has come to an end,
The carnies job is not done, time to tear down, hit the
next spot and do it all again.

THE HITCHHIKER

On the edge of the highway she stands alone.
A cigarette in hand and a duffle bag at her feet, thumb out
another adventure she seeks.
Her backdrop is rolling hills of barley and wheat.
Heading to where she does not know nor she does not care.
There is a lot to see on this stretch deserts mountains and
prairies between here and there.
In this pristine province of Alberta, that she has always
called home.
There are many stops she makes along highway 2 then 16
she takes.
Many places she has yet to have seen, so many small towns
in between.
So much land she has not yet explored~
Not wanting to miss a sight on this hitchhiking tour.
A car stops she hops in the passenger seat.
Her preferred way of travel so many different people she
meets.
They all have their own story what brings them here today.
Most of them thank her for the company on this long
stretch of highway.
Traveling on through the night the driver pulls over it is the
end of this ride.
She thanks him as he drives away she waves goodbye~
The hitchhiker again sticks her thumb out patiently
standing on the side of the road waiting for another ride.

THE SACRED BRAID

Many years the tradition past through out the generations
the ritual will not fade.
Grandmothers, mothers, sisters take care of your hair
thinking good thoughts for you in every strand as they
create the sacred braid.
Passing the teachings and trust on to your bride, explaining
that the braid is made of three important strands.
One is body one is mind the other is spirit.
The braid represents the parts of you, bringing you balance
through it.
Keeping peace in your life as a brave as a man.

THE ARTIST

A blank slate placed before her, of stark white.
A stroke of the brush, the canvas comes alive.
The artist starts with a sunset of the summer's sky.
Blending colors of yellows, pinks and purples with wisps of
white.
Cannot tell where they end where they meet, as she gently
runs the brush through.
A horizon begins to appear, now water so clear and so blue.
A change of the brush, she paints a few spruce and birch
trees.
Creating the landscape around us with ease.
Tapping, cleaning, yet another brush change is made.
Now playing with colors pops out light and shade.
Carefully she adds in the mountain range in front of us.
Catching every shadow and color of the majestic rock.
Placed around it base wildflowers and bush.
Dragging the colors down with a dry brush~
The landscape reflects now cast upon the painted lake.
The painting is worth a 1000 words, better than a picture
you can take.
The details so perfect, the peacefulness she caught.
Never to forget the time we shared at this beautiful vacation
spot.

THE TRUCK DRIVER

Eighteen wheels carry you across country, day and night~
another full load you're hauling.
CB chatter of fellow truckers, cell phone ringing, it's 8 p.m.
your family is calling.
Only fifteen hundred miles to go and then you will be
home.
His wife tells him good night I love you as she hangs up the
phone.
The road is getting longer now, in your sleeper you crawl.
Try to update your logbook, in a deep sleep you fall.
Only a few hours later your up~ check the chains that holds
the load.
Get back in and start the truck, slowly heading out on the
open road.
Through rain and snow you will travel.
Driving down hill, side roads of potholes, ice and gravel.
A treacherous toll it will be.
Miles of ice fog nothing you can see.
Going on instinct and on your gut.
You drive on trusting your truck.
Two more days your destination will be met.
Your truck will be empty and towards home you'll head.
One more day, your road grows shorter.
Now you're three hundred miles west of the Yellowknife
Border.
The load is delivered the truckers job happy that it is
complete.
For the trucker knowing in a few days cradled in his arms
his adoring wife will sleep.

THE FISHERMAN

Cast of the line, the hook skips across the lake.
As the fisherman patiently sits and waits.
This is a special day ~ he is with his son.
This is the day his boy brings in the big one.
Many of legends, stories of lore.
About the 30lb catfish only one man has seen before.
If it is down there this day it will be caught.
Every type of hook and lure this fisherman has brought.
This day is more than fishing it is about building a stronger
bond with his son.
Learning about one another, your likes and dislikes, just
spending a day with your loved one.
In the end it doesn't matter about that fish at the bottom of
the lake.
It was about spending time together a moment nobody can
take.
Another cast of the line, his son's hook skips across the lake.
The Fisherman and his son patiently sit and wait.

THE TRAPPER

Quietly he walks through the woods, not breaking a twig as
he goes.
Walking through the forest, every tree he knows.
For him the paths are like marked city streets.
Over 50 miles a day he travels on his feet.
Checking traps and snares, for his family to feed.
Being sure not taking from nature more than they need.
Through all types of weather he has undergone.
Not letting it stop him the trapper carries on.
He travels past rivers of blue and fields of green.
This world he chose to live in, untouched by man this land
so pristine.
Traveling through bush all throughout the day and night.
Getting closer to his tiny cabin by the morn's light.

THE HUNTER

He raises his rifle in his sites he can see.
As the five point buck steps out from behind the tree.
Ready, aim, hand steady, not a shake.
Wanting to take him down, one shot it should take.
He does not shoot at the buck until he is sure.
Careful not to make a sound, he takes his shot.
With a loud thud the buck falls right there on that spot.
A nice clean shot he's done this before.
To God and Mother Nature he thanks them on bended
knee.
Knowing one more long cold winter his family he can feed.

THE GAMBLER

The gambler is addicted to this Texas Hold'em game.
Thinking it will bring fortune and fame.
The play of the cards is it all luck?
Hoping he will win the next one, down to his last buck.
He holds in his hand the king and ace of clubs.
What happens now depends on the flop.
The dealer flips up a queen, a jack the eight of hearts.
Will his luck be with him, with the next turn of the card?
Not what he wanted instead it is the seven.
Worried, sweat beads form on his forehead,
With hesitation he places his bet.
Keeping his fingers crossed he needs the ten.
On the river it appears, the gambler wins!
The other players not happy, at the sight of his grin.
As he reaches across the table his winnings he collects.
Another round dealt, the gambler places his bet.

THE BULL RIDER

The cowboy adjusts his hat climbs over the stall.
Slowly lowers himself on that animal wild and pure brawn.
Wraps his hand carefully in the rope ~ 8.0 seconds he needs
to hang on.
The gate whips open, the cowboy's head bowed down as the
raging animal bursts out.
The strong power of the muscular structure twisting and
turning throwing the cowboy about.
The red dirt flies up around him swirling in the wind
creating a dusty wall.
The cowboy's head snaps forward then thrusting back; one
hand stays up then a quick twist, the cowboy falls.
7.8 second ride on that angry bull!

STEED YOU RIDE

Nothing can change the magnificent feelings of freedom on
this steed you ride.
Giving you a sense of power, strength and pride.
Propped up on your saddle the sky vibrant and blue,
Free of worries now your world seems bright.
The power of the horse's hooves pounding on the ground—
Drowning out the noise of static of the negativity you hold
inside.
The wind blows through your hair cleansing your soul—
Bringing you inner peace, contentment this majestic animal
invokes.
The world no longer seeming small and dark,
A light appears in your heart.
Once again feeling free and alive,
On this steed you ride.

TAKE A LOOK AROUND

Our lives, our world has altered.
Things are not the same.

Murder, Mayhem, War all around us.
Little children slain.

Do we not see, lost our focus?
Does no one feel shame!

Bullets fly, Knives drawn.
This is where we once played hopscotch on.
These streets now blood stained.

Where does it stop ~ this chaotic blame game.
It's up to us as people to recognize, and stop the pain.

THE EYES OF THE SOUL

Look in the eyes of others,
The eyes of a stranger your friends, family your lover.
See what they see, their moments their world, their feelings.
The eyes say all.
In a quick glance you can see a part of their soul.
They are revealing..
Take notice,
Do not look away.

For you will never know what the eyes may say!

BROTHER OF THE STREET

Perched up against a cold brick wall.
Frost bit hand wrapped around an empty beer bottle.
Face scrapped, clothes ragged, dirty, and torn.
Wondering when did you last eat or slept where it was
warm.
Your eyes dark, vacant and dim.
Something recognizable, telling ourselves " No that's not
him."
I stand in front of you offering you my hand.
Helping you up, I will be here if you fall.
Let me bring you home and release you from the street.
You look at me.. Briefly our eyes meet.
I now see the man I once knew so proud so tall.
Not knowing I am your sister once your best friend.
You push me away, spitting on my hand.
Not giving up on you, I whisper in your ear.
It is ok my brother, It's me your sister, I am here.
A single tear runs down your cheek.
Pushing yourself up now, still wobbly on your feet.
No longer alone you have to fight this battle, my brother of
the street.

BEATEN AND WEAK

A single tear runs down her cheek, dripping off her chin.
Doesn't understand why he beat her once again.
Eye of black and blue yet another fat lip.
Trying to stop the blood from her nose it drips.
This time he really hit her hard, out of control her world
spins.
His voice ringing in her ears, she's ugly and stupid, she's
lucky to have him.
She tells her friends "he didn't mean it, he had a bad day."
She tells them " he loves her true he wasn't always this way."
They plead with her, knowing in their hearts this is a bad
marriage, in it she cannot stay.
She knows in her heart if she tries to leave,
He will do what he can to stop her; scared, from him she
never escapes.
She starts to believe his words, deserving the slaps the kicks.
She must have done something wrong for him to use his
fists.
Things get harder her friends are gone, his plan perfectly
played out.
He has somebody to control it is power he needs.
Nobody left for you to turn to, to hear your cries for help.
Afraid to put him in jail, you continue to live in hell.
Shut off from the world, from her self-esteem.
Left gazing out the window, feeling vacant and alone, barely
able to stand, beaten and weak.

A Child's Cry

A flash of light, a bang, a car speeds by.
A mother jumps to her feet at the sound of her child's cry.
Rushing out her door, a sight of terror on the street.
Lie bleeding her child at her feet.

Neighbors rush to the mother's aid.
Not breathing, too late to save.
Moments ago, riding her bike.
One minute of violence taking her life.
Caught in the middle of another gang fight.

So many questions no answers to bear.
A mother's screams echo, "Life's not fair!"
Turning our streets into a fire zone.
Keeping us all locked in our homes.

Who are these people, what gives them the right to control
our streets, day and night?
A flash of light, a bang, a car speeds by.
Another mother jumps to her feet at the sound of her
child's cry!

WHAT KIND OF WORLD

What kind of world we would have if cobwebs fill the corners of the writers mind covering his door of creativity, his words lost with in the dust?

What kind of world would we have if painter's palette were only gray, with no image to paint and no bristles in the brush?

What kind of world would we have if there were no birds in the sky no bee's in the nest or any scent to a rose?

What kind of world would we have if the photographer had no eye, no images to take because his shutter was permanently closed?

What kind of world would we have if there were no instruments to play no lyrics to sing, no musicians to write a note?

What kind of world would we have if we all gave up on love and hope?

OH BROKEN CHILD

Oh broken child, from here where do you go?
Learning dysfunction, a criminal's world is your home.
A drug dealer's life is all you see.
How can you learn what true happiness can be.
At night you're always hungry~ always frightened~ living
with terror.
Seeing and hearing things most people see in movies of
drama and horror.
Grab your teddy bear and pillow, your safe place with your
brother you hide.
The screaming and the fighting begin, again another bad
night.
Silence for a moment, then it's broken by the sound of a
slap, and a crash.
Surrounding your mother around her feet, shards of broken
glass.
He begins to chuckle such as sadistic laugh.
Dark red drops of her blood splashing up as they hit the
floor.
Screaming at her "Look at this mess, clean it or you will get
more!"
To his chair he mumbles and staggers then sits.
Another beer, another pill, then a cocaine hit.
The house grows silent, your father passes out.
Oh broken child you're to young to know this is not what
life's about.
Now standing before you your mother bleeding and
bruised.

Looking at you and your brother, this is not the life she
wanted to choose.
Quietly the three of you go, never to return.
Oh broken child so much of wrong doings you've seen and
learned.
Can escaping fix the past of dysfunction and chaos.
Or will it always be with you deeply hidden and not forgot.

A BATTERED LIFE

Locked up…forced to hide fears and tears.
Locked up…behind cold windowpanes.
All because of his joys, thrills and psychotic games.

While he enjoyed the fight.
He could not handle the hurt the tears.
Only bringing hell into the night.
Soon turning my nightmares into the living.
Making me do all the work all the giving.

STOP THE SCREAMING STOP THE HITTING,
STOP THE FEAR!

Now all I see is a scared little girl in the mirror.
Once I was a woman, now a child
Trying to be again, it will take awhile.
Afraid of people and feelings of love
Hoping, praying one day all of this I can rise above.

No Longer Your Victim

Your family became blended; you became her brother that is when the horrors began.

Being a small child the things you were doing she did not understand.

The pain you inflicted permanently damaging a part of her soul.

Every night she was afraid to sleep, during the day afraid to be at home.

You threw boulders and rubble on the path she had before her.

You took so much from her, her dignity her virginity, destroying her inside removing her chances of having a baby.

You were caught once they told you never to touch her again from now on you were to leave her alone.

That made things worse, more aggressive things became injuring her in places unable to show.

For a long time she was afraid to tell ~ convincing herself it was her fault she deserved this punishment you condemned her to hell.

Able to split herself as she laid there watching what you were doing to her, with a tear filled eye crying for the little girl she sees.

Drifting away from her inner light, numbness was left she was no longer a little girl inside.

Nothing left but an outside layer of a shattered scared confused tired and weak shell that is fragile and ready to break.

She learned how to build a wall behind it hid what you did. Protected by shame, guarded with untrue emotions dressed in fake smiles.

She was happy when you left the house you went off with a wife and had kids.

Thought things would change for her, maybe she had a chance.

Not having the opportunity to corner her again, you still grabbed groped and pinched.

You always found ways to put her down, able to make her feel she was not a part of the family whenever you came around.

Always doing your best to show her that she did not belong.

She left home at a young age not able to deal with the guilt the shame the hate.

She was so rebellious and angry, reflecting it on to those that did not see your abuse; it was them she started to blame.

Realizing later she was living the life that you said she deserved and would choose.

You put her in a dark place and left her there for a long time, left alone to die or to stand and fight.

It took a lot of work and struggles for her to find a light and leave the darkness of anger and hurt behind.

She uncovered the damnation you piled on her found underneath what made her strong.

She is no longer your victim you are no longer in control.

She is now the master of her life and has healed her soul.

So each night she prays that other's will never endure the pain you once made her feel.

THE FALLEN FAMILY

The neighborhood and local news teams encircle the tiny
house of blue and white.
The pristine flowerbed of petunias and germaniums lit up
by all the photographer's cameras flashing lights.
Everyone is trying to get a look at the disturbing sight.
Not being able to fathom the shocking horror inside.
This morbid curiosity will not be satisfied as yellow police
tape borders the flawless manicured lawn.
The home the most inviting on the block now closed off the
curtains drawn.
An eerie sight, the first step through the doorway~
A young officer runs out the scene too much for him to
convey.
First a small trail of splatter leading to a dark pool of blood,
lying in the middle the young mother and wife.
Stabbed more than they can count, in her back remains the
knife.
As the team of policemen move through the house none of
them prepared for what they are about to see.
Two small innocent sisters shot where they sleep~
The blood stained feather pillows still placed over their
heads.
Many of these men have never seen anything like it.
All the training they've had can't hold a candle to this.
The image they will always hold, never understanding the
horror in front of them finding it hard to come to grips.
Down at the end of the hall the husband they find, a gun at
his feet shot himself in the face.

117

No reasons for his madness, scribbled on a note pad the words I'm sorry, my family I've disgraced.
No one could find the answers to what happened here that day,
At this tiny little house of blue and white, where once all you heard was with the joyous sound of children at play.
Neighbors now stand in shock realizing no longer any laughter will fill the yard, now just an anomalous silence as the coroner hauls four body bags away.

WHERE DID YOU GO

There you sit with your crack pipe..
Propped up in a corner, back to the wall.
Just one more hit.. Then everything will be alright.
Erasing memories your world now so small.
Giving up family, dignity and pride.
You crawl inside yourself, from reality you hide.
Not seeing how we all worry, that we care.
The person we all once knew is no longer there.

THE ROAD TRIP

Car loaded, the teens pile in ~
Equipped with road pops, munchies and happy sticks, their
adventure begins.
The time 4:20, highway destination ~ nowhere!
No thoughts about life ahead of them, free spirited no
worries, no cares.
The tires and passengers blazing heading towards the sun.
Creating a memory~ forever cherish this moment to it hold
on.
The snap the fizz a familiar sound to them the music of the
road pop, another one opened ~the car now in high gear.
Nothing fazing the young driver ~ he has another beer.
All they have is this moment~ the road they are about to
approach is to be bumpy and long…
As a logging truck bears around the corner,
The teen driver that was just having fun hits the truck dead
on!

JUST A THOUGHT

You can't find the light unless you've seen the dark.
You can't feel the pain without experiencing the hurt.
You can't complete a contract without the coming together
of the minds.
You can't learn to grow if you don't plant the seed.
You can't write words of wisdom if you have no knowledge.
You can't learn to tread water then swim if you are afraid to
get in.
You can't give an answer to a question that has never been
asked.
Self-doubt can drive you forward, finding no flaws will hold
you back.
The ride of life is quick and fast, so with open eyes take a
firm grasp.
Try not to figure out the meaning of life, once you do you
quit living, you distinguish your light.

SMOKE AND STALE BEER

You'll find all types of people here,
In this dim lit room, smell of smoke and stale beer.
The crack of the break, as the pool balls scatter.
Room filled with conversation and laughter.
Off in the corner you see body's sway,
Dancing to the creative selection the DJ plays.
Candle on the table set for two~
They're not seeing anyone else in the room.
Bells go off it's the ringing of the VLT's ~ 7's just hit.
Wondering if they should keep playing or be smart and
quit!
The waitress keeps serving, fast and light on her feet.
Making sure to tend to all her customer's needs.
The lonely old widower who's second home is the bar.
The stage and the spotlight are for the Karaoke star.
The girl, whom had too much to drink,
Her once perfect make-up now running looks like black
ink.
The lonely people gaze across the room, their eyes meet.
Is this the one true love they seek?
Two best buddies go from laughing to fists flying,
While a group of women console their friend, who is
crying.
The hardworking stiff needs to relax, arrives late.
A couple sitting awkwardly, another bad blind date.

Every night the bartender sees them here.
In this dim lit room, smell of smoke and stale beer.

COSMETIC SURGERY.

What happened to growing old gracefully?
Women that are fifty are trying to look thirty.
Choosing youth over reality, can't accept young years you've
past.
Cosmetic surgery~ how long can this fad last!
Lips injected, foreheads frozen, lines diminished.
Look ten years younger still your not finished.
Breast implants will they make you feel better?
People no longer looking at your face, just at your sweater.
Butt lifts and tummy tucks to make you thin.
Where does the real you start and the plastic begin?
Another appointment you make, another procedure you
under go.
When are you going to let go of your youth, and find it's
great growing old!

.

AUSCHWITZ

The strong and the young chosen were for slave labor.
Mothers, children and the elderly were chosen for murder.
Marched in orderly fashion to the Nazi's gas chamber.
Showing the world that hell does exist.
Here in the place known as Auschwitz.

Killing of friends and families, one hundred Jews were
ordered to assist.
Collecting the bodies, having to carry them to ovens and
open pits.
Showing the world that hell does exist.
Here in the place known as Auschwitz.

Everyday the smell of burnt flesh and ash filled the air.
Waking to the sound of gunshots ~ men assassinated, shot
behind the ear.
Showing the world that hell does exist.
Here in this place known as Auschwitz.

Starved for not only food, but also human kindness~
looking to the heavens above.
Feelings of being abandoned and forgotten, by man of war
and God.
Showing the world that hell does exist.
Here in this place known as Auschwitz.

Over four hundred fifty thousand lives ~ souls were stolen
in this place.

All stemming from racism and hate.
Forever affecting millions of people, their family history, their fate.
Showing the world that hell does exist.
Here in this place known as Auschwitz.
We have to never forget...
The terror these people met.
Remind people hell does exist.
Just see what happened here, in this place known as Auschwitz.

WILLIAM KIDD

Born about 1645.
Becoming one of the greatest pirates of our times.
King appointed him captain of his own ship.
The Adventure Galley, crew of 80 and 34 cannons, she was
equipped.
Your job ~ capture all the French and Pirates of Madagascar.
Picking a better crew a gang of cutthroats that is where your
story starts.
A mutiny occurs some of your crew decided to jump ship.
" Attack all or any" " Or that will be it!"
A fight broke out with the ships gunner ~refusing the
mutiny at hand.
Kidd's life changed the day he killed that man.
Plundering ships now, for bounty for treasure.
Sailing up closely throwing grappling hooks bring the two
ships together.
Quedagh Merchant, carrying 400 tons of treasure, Kidd's
for the taking, the bigger ship at his surrender.
Captain William Kidd possessed one of the greatest pirate
treasures ever.
Stealing from those who set him on the waters to sail.
There was to be a hanging, noose broke twice the third not
to fail.
His body served as a warning for all Pirates to come.
After his death dipped in tar wrapped in chains, along the
river he hung.

LOST SOLDIERS

Lost soldiers, forgotten souls.
The sacrifices they made for us.
Their stories can never be untold.

Fighting for our freedom-
Crawling and sleeping in the cold wet mud
Day after day, night after night.
Over their heads bullets fly.
Hitler's buzz saw blazing steadily at our brothers, sons, and
friends.
Our boys our men!
The roar of the tiger tanks rumbling up from behind.
A flash of his family runs through his mind.

The battles they've seen the battles they endured.
For us, for our future to be secure.
Many have lost their lives never to return home.
Lost soldiers, my brothers, my friends.
Your stories will be told,
Our brave soldiers, our brave men!

A Soldier's Letter

Equipped with a pen and words from the heart,
Not knowing what to say, where does he start?
A tear in his eye, he begins to write his letter.
By thanking his family for the life, the love they shared
together.
With trembling hand his words of admiration for his
parents pour out.
Letting them know in his short life he had no regrets, no
doubts.
Requesting them do not to shed a tear, for him do not be
sad.
At home he was a boy, here a man, proud of the soldier's
life he had.
Picturing his family faces, their world crumbles; he can hear
his mother's cry.
Neatly he folds the paper up, praying his unit never has to
send this letter of goodbye.

ERADICATE YOUR HATRED

Eradicate your hatred spew it from within.
The empathic part of your soul abandoned.
As to be placed in the thick, damp ominous rain forest.
The malaria infested mosquitoes not the threat.
Surrounded by snipers, land mines, and steps away full of
hostels a POW camp.
The captured; your sense of human kindness and
understanding.
The war within yourself.
Your hate encumbers any decency you may have left.
Now is the time to fight for the survival of your
personification.
Allow the unequivocal resistance of your dignity to step in.
Step in to rescue you from the hatred you hold within.

THE BATTLE

An all day effort, accomplishments many, lessons
learned, moments of laughter shared.
One another's construction slightly differs~ both
having the same purpose.
A place of protection they built with special care.
Working together on their shelters as they prepare
for warfare.

The weather is changing the sky turns dusk.
Not much more they can do today still they try hard
to beat the clock.
They watch each other from across the field with
tomorrow weighing heavily on their minds neither
speaks.
Tomorrow is D Day this is their last night of peace.

Dawn arrives the air is crisp the sky is clear.
They glare at one another knowing the battle is near.
They prepare for combat each has been on this field
before.
Wishing the other one with a sarcastic "good luck!"
they trek off to their separate forts.

The terrain is a tough one made of snow and ice.

They know what is in store, its not going to be an easy fight.
They duck in behind the walls they carved out yesterday.
Checking their artillery they both establish they are ready.
The battle begins ~ it can go either way.

It is brother against sister, which one will prevail?
They fire upon one another hitting the shelter's sides.
Trying to find the weak spots so the opponent has nowhere to hide.
As they plummet one another ~ the day, the battle goes on forever~

Establishing victory and control of the yard he will hold all the power.
At least for a while until mom calls them in for the night.
Ending another great snowball fight.

How Do You Stop The War Of....

How do you stop the war of racism, humanity and understanding are the soldiers to deploy.

How to stop war of violence against one another, combat it with compassion and the ability to listen ~ placed on the front lines ready for action, supporting humanity and understanding.

How do you stop the war of ignorance, join the resistance against hatred and skepticism, backing up compassion, the ability to listen, humanity and understanding.

Coat of Armour an open mind and the willingness to learn.

A launch of ballistic missiles made of thoughtfulness and kind words.

The weapons you carry in this war ~ Love, tolerance and consideration.

THE MEMORY LIBRARY

Row upon row stacked in far-reaching order some never to
reiterate.
Some covered with dust and webs these random thoughts
scattered and displaced.
Hours and Hours… seeming like only seconds wandering
around the memory library.
Chapter after chapter page after page held in illustration
and verse a life's history.
Some guarded by your defense behind an inner brick wall
under lock and key.
There are few checked out, often, corners missing from
constant ear- marks~ the pages wrinkled and worn.
These chapters always to create a smile and any heart it will
warm.
This is the common sitting area made of comfort and free-
living memories surrounded by volumes of adventurous
literature.
These volumes they created together united by the
moments they shared.
New thoughts join the group now working on pages to
review in the near future.
It's closing time now ~ adding more comfort to the chaos
that creates yourself.
The librarian adds new additions and restocks the shelves.
Bring an end to another day spent in the memory library.

Printed in the United States
129990LV00002B/7-30/P